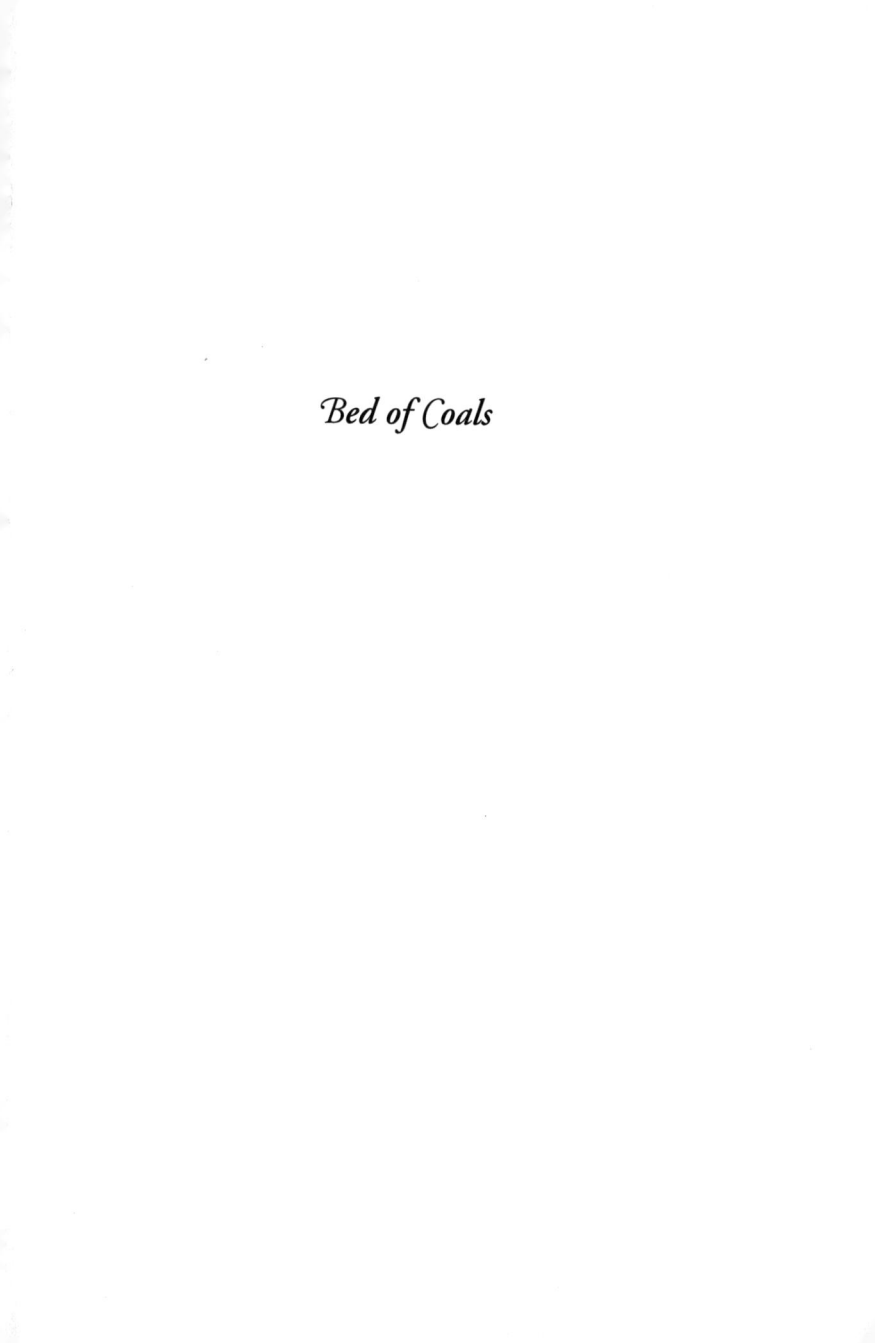

Bed of Coals

Bed of Coals

POEMS BY

Joseph Hutchison

UNIVERSITY PRESS OF COLORADO

© 1995 by the University Press of Colorado
Published by the University Press of Colorado
P. O. Box 849
Niwot, Colorado 80544

All rights reserved. Printed in the United States of America.

The University Press of Colorado is a cooperative publishing enterprise supported, in part, by Adams State College, Colorado State University, Fort Lewis College, Mesa State College, Metropolitan State College of Denver, University of Colorado, University of Northern Colorado, University of Southern Colorado, and Western State College of Colorado.

Acknowledgments

The author gratefully acknowledges the following publications in which poems in this volume first appeared.

Catalyst: "Couplets"
Communiqué: "Vander Meer's Weariness"
The Denver Quarterly: "Vander Meer Crying Fowl" and "Saint Vander Meer and the Dragon"
The Eleventh Muse: "Fullness" and "Awakenings"
Grasshopper: "A Dream"
High Plains Literary Review: "Journey With Music"
Hubbub: "Black Waters" and "Drunk Again in the Dark Grass"
Images: "Long Distance Call"
Kansas Quarterly: "Vander Meer at Sundown"

Louisville Review: "From an Unmailed Letter"

Mississippi Review: "Elemental Prayer in a Black Hour," "Lethe," and "Recalling the Solstice"

Poetry (Chicago): "Shadowy Trees" and "The Wound"

Prism International: "Chinook at Midnight"

Riverstone: "Sword Swallower" and "A Wakeful Night"

South Coast Poetry Journal: "November 10" (under the title "October Rain")

Tar River Poetry: "Vander Meer's Revision," "June 3" (under the title "Blue Recitation"), "Summer Storm," and "The Ache"

Tendril: "Vander Meer Holding On"

Writers Forum: "Ghazal," "The Stone Forest," and "This Day"

Zone 3: "The Effects of Light," "Vander Meer," and "Vander Meer in Transit"

"A Box of Snapshots Unearthed in the Basement" in the anthology *American Dream*, edited by Jim Villani (Pig Iron Press, 1995).

"June 20: 'Lifting My Daughter'" appears as "Lifting My Daughter" in my collection entitled *House of Mirrors* (James Andrews & Co., Publishers, 1992).

"On Opening the Blue Notebook" appears as "Wheelwork" in the anthology *Movieworks* (Little Theatre Press, 1990).

"Vander Meer's Duplicity," "Vander Meer Larger than Life," and "Vander Meer at Bottom" appear in *Tracks in the Snow: Essays by Colorado Poets* (Mesilla Press, 1989).

"One of the Lost Moments" appears in the anthology *Wingbone: Poetry from Colorado* (Sudden Jungle Press, 1986).

"May 21" appears as "The Crosswalk" in a chapbook entitled *Thirst* (Juniper Press, 1984).

Excerpt from "Reluctance" is taken from *The Poetry of Robert Frost,* edited by Edward Connery Lathem, published by Holt Rinehart, 1969.

Library of Congress Cataloging-in-Publication Data

Hutchison, Joseph.
    Bed of coals : poems / by Joseph Hutchison.
      p. cm.
    ISBN 0-87081-374-9 (acid-free paper)
    I. Title.
  PS3558.U834B43   1995
  811'.54—dc20   95-6302
                                                                                                              CIP

This book was set in Adobe Garamond.

The paper used in this publication meets the minimum requirements of the American National Standard for Information Sciences—Permanence of Paper for Printed Library Materials. ANSI Z39.48–1948
∞

10   9   8   7   6   5   4   3   2   1

For Joe Nigg

and, as always,

For Melody

Contents

Author's Note	XIII
Vander Meer	1
Vander Meer's Weariness	3
Vander Meer Larger than Life	4
Vander Meer in Transit	6
On Opening the Blue Notebook	8
From the Blue Notebook:	
July 15: "Con Brio"	9
July 9	10
June 12: "Long Distance Call"	11
Fighting Grief	13
Orphic Vander Meer	14
The Stone Forest	16
Against Remembrance	17
Lethe	18
Vander Meer's Revision	20
The Comforter	22

From the Blue Notebook:
    March 22 23
    April 27: "Couplets" 24
    May 11: "Sword Swallower" 25
    May 21 26
    June 3 27
    June 20: "Lifting My Daughter" 28
    July 22: "Buying the Divorce-Mobile" 29
A Box of Snapshots Unearthed in the Basement 31
Vander Meer Holding On 32
Pausing Outside My Apartment 34
The Effects of Light 35
One of the Lost Moments 37
Summer Storm 38
Journey With Music 39
Vander Meer Crying Fowl 40
Drunk Again in the Dark Grass 41
From the Blue Notebook:
    August 8: "Abstinence" 43
    August 13 44
    September 23 45
    October 19 46
    November 10 47
    December 22: "Withdrawal" 48

A Dream	49
A Wakeful Night	50
Saint Vander Meer and the Dragon	51
Recalling the Solstice	53

From the Blue Notebook:

January 29	54
February 14: "Ghazal"	56
February 20	57
February 23	58
February 28	59
March 10: "From an Unmailed Letter"	60
The Ache	62
Snapshots	63
Vander Meer at Sundown	65
Bed of Coals	66
Vander Meer at Sea	67
Black Waters	69

From the Blue Notebook:

March 21: "Elemental Prayer in a Black Hour"	70
Vander Meer at Bottom	72
The Dazzle	74
Awakenings	75
Fullness	76
The Wound	77

Vander Meer's Duplicity	78
Beyond Sorrow	80
Chinook at Midnight	82
The Voice of Reason	83
This Day	84

Author's Note

Two different voices tell the following story. One belongs to an anonymous narrator, whose poems all include my main character's name—Vander Meer—in their titles. The second voice is Vander Meer's own, and it surfaces in poems drawn from his "blue notebook" and in others written at a later date. His "blue notebook" entries are dated (from March 22 of one year to March 21 of the next) and presented in the order Vander Meer himself chooses to read them. Readers who prefer plot to character are free to reconstruct the progress of Vander Meer's crisis by reading the "blue notebook" poems in chronological order.

Bed of Coals

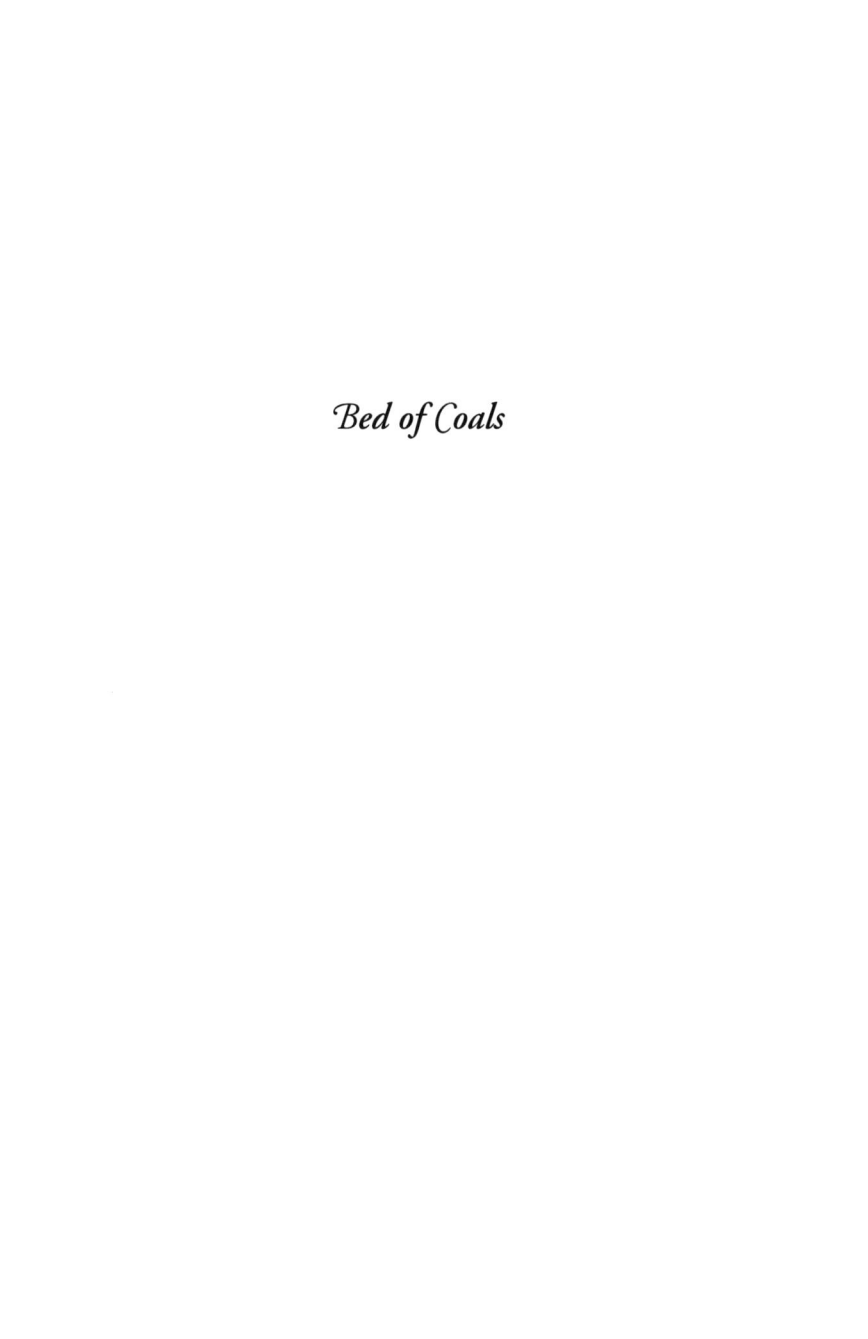

What do definitions and divorce-court proceedings
have to do with the breathless reality?
—Louis Simpson

Now I have already mentioned that there was a disturbance in my
heart, a voice that spoke there and said, *I want, I want, I want!*
—Saul Bellow

> Ah, when to the heart of man
>   Was it ever less than a treason
> To go with the drift of things,
>   To yield with a grace to reason,
> And bow and accept the end
>   Of a love or a season?
> —Robert Frost

Vander Meer

A writer of "copy," that's Vander Meer:
direct mail letters, video scripts—
though he fancies himself an *auteur*.
                                            Daily,
the early bus shakes his big dreams down
and disperses them through the tires,
into the street . . . delivering him up
to work, safely asleep.
                              Some clear mornings,
the routine revives his childhood fear:
learning to swim. . . .

*

There: gulping air, though arms
sustain him . . . choking on
wavelets, the chlorine's cold sting
deep in the bones of his face.
                                     "All right,"
snaps the lean instructor, heaving him
onto the concrete poolside. "You let me know
when you're ready to *try*."
                              So he sits,

gooseflesh blue, till his shameful sense
of being cast out sirens him back—
and against his better judgement
he learns how to float, how to kick,
how to hold his breath. . . .

*

Finally, muses Vander Meer, *every skill
becomes second nature* . . . as the bus
sighs to his stop. And before he knows it
he's up,
        down the steps,
                    out the doors,
on the walk . . . doing his tight little
breast-stroke through the crowd.

Vander Meer's Weariness

Vander Meer's colleagues say he's not himself.
His clear, blue sky prose is all fog lately:
"Couldn't sell steaks to a starving man!"
In meetings, the tall windows draw his gaze—
worse than dozing, his leaves of absence.

Leaves of absence . . . O Walt Whitman!
Who will take Vander Meer now in hand? Who,
O reader of brochures, will discover the ache
staring out through the fretwork of print?

Questions too moot to suit Vander Meer,
weary as he is of such, such as: "Why live?"
Why ask? He trusts in no one who would answer.

VANDER MEER LARGER THAN LIFE

Vander Meer at the roadside—
dust, gravel, a faint wind, locusts
like dry knuckles cracking in the weeds.
Looking down at his empty hands, he
recognizes the haggard blue suit—
North by Northwest: he is Cary Grant.

When you find yourself in an old movie,
you know it's a dream. But the plane
swooping low out of the vacant sky,
roaring over the flattest land on earth—
it makes you wonder . . . makes Vander Meer
hit the dirt as those wing-shadows pour
over him like breath. . . .
                                          And somewhere
inside him, or inside us all, the great
stone heads of Rushmore are rising
out of the dark like Leviathans—brows
and cheeks we cling to, as primitives
cling to the gods that dwarf them.

No wonder we awaken like Vander Meer!
Weary, aching, a second-rate actor
in the White House . . . and the sun

like some film projector, briefing
our sleep with its dream-laden
whisper of broken light. . . .

Vander Meer in Transit

Riding the downtown bus, he overheard
two women. The younger, in cape and cocked
beret, spoke intently to the one in blue.

"I took a night course on dreaming,"
she said. "If you dream it once,
it's not prophetic. It's just working out
anxieties. . . ."
                    "And what if you dream
the dream more than once?"
                              "Then,"
she nodded, "it's time to pay attention."

The conversation cracked Vander Meer up—
till he thought back to the nightmare
in which his penis, a limp pouch
plump with pale custard, tore away
in the shower . . . and instead
of a cock he had a bright red
stick, gnarled as a crone's finger,
erect in the rain (for he was suddenly
outside in angry weather, paralyzed
by fear of lightning). . . .
                              Vander Meer

shuddered . . . or the bus shuddered,
braking. He'd dreamed that often,
two years before his marriage failed.

A tap on his shoulder. "Isn't this where you
get off?" the young woman asked.
                              "No,"
Vander Meer smiled. Her cape, as she turned,
swept by his abstracted eyes like a dark,
heavy wind. . . .
              Today he would call in
sick. Yes. But first he would ride
clear to the end of the line.

On Opening the Blue Notebook

Victor/Victoria on the VCR: miss a line,
stop tape and rewind, play it again—
our technology of second chances.
When I picture you, I hear
such gears engage—as if thought
were a kind of wheelwork, routinely
spinning dreams into images,
love into dreams. . . .
And it is: the past, badly edited,
flickers away inside us; now
is a vast raw footage; the future,
hissing snow if we prematurely
try to play it through.
The screen in my head shows you,
and you, and you again—legs
hugging me, my name quick
on your breath . . . till I long
to enter the picture, the circuits
of loss; at any cost to grasp
what you were, what you've become:
light, and the charged residue of light.

July 15: "Con Brio"

Too treble for ears, a gracenote's summons
feathered through our brains, piped us
to the pied guestbed quilt. Spreading towels
against stain, she baptized my bald homage
in water holy past pun or punishment. Our method—
pure rhythm; as a rosined bow thrills the gut
to gladden the soul, so the lingua franca,
pentecostal stammering of our hearts
renewed us. Spouses, friends, hurt families
only meant we'd need to stop and think—
someday. Not then. Blind joy with its wings
of breath raised us up (though I'm no Christian,
and in her the Pope's crosier had dwindled
from flute to pennywhistle) . . . raised us up
catholic, graceful con brio *and fluent in tongues.*

JULY 9

*In bed we listened
to sleepwalking rain
drawn to the window
by your wetness*

June 21: "Long Distance Call"

From a tangle of wires your voice
touches me
like a breeze reaching
through a screen some morning
of intense summer
so that I find myself
listening
to the way your lips
meet and part
how your tongue shapes
out of breath the language I love

until I know it is
one breath
lifting your words and mine
one breath shared through the wires
until every distance between us
dwindles and we
feel our charged voices
pulsing over lakes and fields
over hill after hill
inside us now
drawing us into a room
where we lie moving
slowly at first

*tongue to tongue
in the house of longing*

*whose every window
opens on a fresh dawn wind
on a sky of white clouds sailing
on birch shadows swimming
in blowing grass
the bright curtains stirring
like our own moist bodies*

everything breathing together

Fighting Grief

We shared a shower, talking
and touching, the morning
after our first night together.
We kept it cool because of the heat.
I felt whole, my cough was gone,
her breasts were slippery
in my soapy hands.
The water that sprayed us
her husband owned: spray, soap,
tub and house. Only the day
was not his to keep—
our bodies, our voices,
touching and talking.
That's why, fighting grief,
I remember her wet belly pressed
against mine, her dripping
hair, the precarious
joy I felt as she gently
wiped me dry with his towel.

ORPHIC VANDER MEER

As he entered her body, the first time,
she wept—but not with joy. Tremors
ringing out from her collapsing marriage
shuddered through them both. He didn't know,
but guessed the Church was crumbling too,
and the colossus she called Mother.

                              Shaken
Vander Meer! Probing her past for the ruins
he might restore, raise up in new shapes,
new shelter. Yet how dumb he looked
in khakis, boots and pith, shouldering
a pick-ax in place of a lyre. Myopic, all
catalogs and theories, archaeologist
of love.

       No wonder she's withdrawn—
gone darkly like Eurydice—to engineer
her own new life. Was it his backward look?
Or did she bow to a deep necessity?

                                  Well,
it scarcely matters now to Vander Meer,
tossing on his bed, lost head borne
on the white wave of his pillow. Adrift
in his dream, perhaps he can remember

himself, discover a cure-all voice
to raise above the bloody lamentation
of his heart.
         Of course, we may forgive
pragmatists and Christians if they doubt it.

THE STONE FOREST

Love threads upward in the numb root of the spine:
luminous water, its origins dark. And marriages

fall to their knees as the red leaves unfurl,
bright in the back of the mind, with a rich

rustling sound like surf at night. But the sea,
we soon find, is far away; the sound's only wind.

The wounded heart wakens again in the stone forest.

Against Remembrance

Patches of brightness throb on the water:
faces, fingerings, open mouths, ghosts.
They hurt the eye that keeps on watching,
the heart that keeps growing darker anyhow.

LETHE

"You pulled back," she said. "You were so
passionate, and then you were gone."
The sky curved above their house like a tree,
ash or willow, thick-leaved, many-branched.
She said, "Is there anything wrong?"

He stood at the window. Full moonlight
bleached his bare arms and the patch
of April snow, grave-shaped, out in the yard.
Words that had forced his lips as he moved
upon her body like a furious stream
he'd meant for another—say that moon—
and they'd left him bewildered.

He thought, *What could be wrong?*

At times the spirit-bag he wore, tied
inside his chest with an artery and a vein,
radiated healing, and at times was a coal
brightening and scorching with every breath,
and was sometimes a heart that knew how to love,
and sometimes it was a faithless heart.

"What could be wrong?" he said.

But sleep had come over her like snow,
like the shade of a spreading tree.
Her breathing flooded the room.

Lethe, he thought. *Amen.*

Vander Meer's Revision

Discovering another man's words crept
in among his own, Vander Meer dutifully
strikes them. (Though writing for himself,
he likes to make it new.) But the pruned
phrase—"The energy leaves the wine"—
makes his memory wander. . . .

                                        August;
a night-wind enriched by the moist grass
he hadn't mowed in weeks . . . and crickets!
Thick as stars in the yard. He is reading
in the half-dark, angled over the book
like a slab face on Easter Island, mouth
slight-moving: "The energy leaves the wine,"
thinking: *But there are reasons.*

                                            And yet,
one August later he was living alone—
three floors up, leaning half-naked
into the open jaws of a panting fridge,
letting it lap his sweat away. Off and on
her voice would drum again in his ears:
"You want her? Your little bitch? *Go*
to her! *Go to your bitch!*"

                                        So he left,

not explaining he was leaving for no one.
How could he speak that unreasonable truth?
"The energy leaves the wine," and the god
wakes in you no longer . . . no longer
takes wing suddenly in your blood—
and your own voice sours in your mouth,
and your best words. . . .
                        Speechless
Vander Meer! Reeling again . . . flushed
like some sullen, intemperate priest,
drunk as a lord on the sacrament.

The Comforter

The new comforter, unfamiliarly rumpled,
dreamed itself suddenly into a shape—
her shape—and the thread of my breath
snagged . . . for a heartbeat hung me up,
till I saw that she was really just
an absence in my bed. . . .

I wandered into the furnace room,
sat on a box of clothing we'd packed
for Goodwill or the Salvation Army.
Tented in drying laundry, I drank in
the hushed uproar of the gas, grief
weaving in my arteries like gin
or my 80 proof adolescence.

Then my wife walked in, glanced
down . . . and somberly gathered up
the permanent press shirts still
stubbornly wrinkled, the ones
she'd iron in the gray TV light:
shoving the Sunbeam back and forth
amid music, gunfire, canned laughter—
smoothing the folds, her cheeks gleaming.

March 22

STOP SLAUGHTERING BABY SEALS or NO MORE NUKES—
pathos of loving what we can't love enough.
"When they split up," some voice at the office,
"he joined The Alliance to Protect Snail Darters.
She worked door-to-door for Z.P.G." Today,
following a night of smashed glasses
and food-slopped floors, our three-year-old
stared down my bitter breakfast silence:
"You're not screaming now." My eyes burned wet
as an oil-slicked dolphin's. . . . Where are you,
Committee to Preserve Self-Devouring Spouses?
Yet I have kissed her mouth most tenderly—
mouth, breasts, curve of belly . . . cavorting
in a surf of sheets. And later, breathing
to sleep in the depths, I've dreamed in slogans:
No More Nukes! Stop the Slaughter! Save the Whales!

April 27: "Couplets"

*He is rooted inside her, his breath branching out
heavy with leaves: the dark names he calls her.*

*

*A shallow light streaming from the TV. Drowned,
they touch like fugitives breathing through straws.*

*

*The glass he lifts holds her face, inverted:
she frowns, as if he is drunk on wine.*

*

Slapping his own face: Brut. *Then the drain
chuckles, chokes . . . stutters his secret name.*

*

*Lying by her in April sun, remote—how he envies
the bee like a flame in the folds of its rose!*

May 11: "Sword Swallower"

*The arm-long blade glides down my gaping throat;
rubes drop their popcorn to clap. . . . This damned
carnival! My life . . . sawdust and rigged wheels,
the shellgames intellect plays with desire—
"A fortune under every shell!" the barker growls.
My audience, believing it, drifts off. I draw
the steel out carefully then, so as not to slice
my heart . . . but its form remains—a keening
edge in everything I say. . . . Yet I go on
performing the great illusion of conversation!
The weapon in my banter flashes, I laugh or weep—
and talking to myself, I bleed. . . . My art's
all irony: a real sword seems to wound, an imagined
wounds for real. I trust in nothing but my skill,
knowing my faith is a rube's: every wheel is rigged;
the shell we pick is never the shell our fortune's under.*

May 21

It's a lightpole at a city crosswalk. Over the grit, someone has scrawled with a black magic marker: JESUS, SAVE MY SOUL. Traffic like cold wind. You lean into it, the way you lean a while later into the chilly fluorescence at your desk. That beetle glimpsed as it vanished into a sidewalk crack—with a start, you realize it lives there. A tremor takes your hand like cicadas grinding up time in the willows. Weren't there days when horizons, at dawn or at dusk, shone like a Bible's gilt edge? Then where did these nights come from? Nights you dream of nothing but the crosswalk downtown: how the signal keeps changing—WALK, DON'T WALK—though no one is there to cross and the street itself is empty.

JUNE 3

*Here is the valley: green slopes, naked
peaks splotched with obstinate snow.*

*Below us, the river's froth and dazzle—
a blue recitation from* The Book of Changes.

*We're at ease together almost an hour
amid all this perishable splendor.*

*

*Back in the car, it's a hundred miles
to what's left of home: walls and a roof.*

*Then nightfall. The mountains invisible,
their summits and canyons withdrawn.*

*But sinking to sleep we hear the river:
a blue recitation from* The Book of Changes.

June 20: "Lifting My Daughter"

*As I leave for work she holds out her arms, and I
bend to lift her . . . always heavier than I remember,
because in my mind she is still that seedling bough
I used to cradle in one elbow. Her hug is honest,
fierce, forgiving. I think of Oregon's coastal pines,
wind-bent even on quiet days; they've grown in ways
the Pacific breeze has blown them all their lives.
And how will my daughter grow? Last night, I dreamed
of a mid-ocean gale, a howl among writhing waterspouts;
I don't know what it meant, or if it's still distant,
or already here. I know only how I hug my daughter,
my arms grown taut with the thought of that wind.*

July 22: "Buying the Divorce-Mobile"

*The smashed headlamp makes the whole front
look wall-eyed, and the dented left door
winces like a pockmarked cheek. I can't believe
I'm thinking this, anthropomorphically I mean,
but the car's as pitiful as certain girls
in hand-me-down prom dresses (hornrims thick
as depression glass) and the vague, half
hopeful, off-the-other-way looks they
listen to dance music with. It's listening
too, this beat-up blue car for sale so cheap
I've already figured I might need to wire
the muffler up with a bent coat-hanger—
an idea I don't announce. The pretty owner
(whose tattooed boyfriend just roared off
for "beer and smokes" on the long throb
of his Harley) clearly still cares, aches
to sell and not sell. But here on the ridge
above the snarling freeway, money's tight;
she needs to shake some loose from me.
"It drives good," she says. "And y'know
how great Bugs are in snow. It's been real
nice, 'cause believe me this hill's the last
road on earth they bother to plow." I touch
the torn fender, the cracked side mirror,*

*amazed that this is what I'm worth—me,
my first good job and one broken marriage
into a life that will end. I look at her
hard, counting the costs, and she looks
off the other way. I feel darkness dancing
in my veins. "All right. I'll take it," I say.*

A Box of Snapshots Unearthed in the Basement

In these old photos it's always me
as I am, but with memories added:
an awareness of how things went
after this bearded grin faded,
after that wedding cake was cut.
But the past isn't sad; it's

simply gone—though the face
in these snaps is always mine
as I picture it even now (when
not staring into a mirror):
passably human, almost alert.
And yet I have slumbered my way

through most of it; and sleep now,
I suppose. Since it's me as I am
in the willow tree's shadow, me
in the shade of my parent's house—
but lit by a knowledge so bright
I have to shut my eyes to see.

Vander Meer Holding On

Slouched behind the wheel of his new
used Ford, Vander Meer sights down the gap
between his ex-house and the neighbors'.

A view of the swingset he assembled,
skinning his knuckles all the raw morning
and howling, "Why the hell do we *never*
have the right tools?" Now his daughter's
swinging there, clinging to the chains.
Off and on, a glimpse of his wife—
shoving . . . making the child's hair
float out behind her like blown cornsilk.

It all reminds him of his own swinging youth:
the way ground seesawed as he pumped, head
thrown so far back his vision hung trees
by their heels from a heaven of grass!
And the buoyant tug of links in his hands,
tug of the pulse in his eyes . . . so strong
he believed he could always let his body
flirt with such sweet falling. . . .

But his daughter, sailing higher, shrieks
with joy . . . and he grips the wheel—
white-knuckled Vander Meer! Shutting his eyes,
hearing his wife laugh and call, "Hold on!
Honey, hold on tight!" Her every push
pushing him farther out. . . .

Pausing Outside My Apartment

Sun must be filling the room.
A bright ray is streaming
from the peephole.

Daylight and dust.

You can feel the earth
turning under you at times.
The roundness of anguish.

Daylight and dust.

It's like a dream.
The key turns my hand.
I open my life and go in.

The Effects of Light

I've tacked Vermeer's
Girl in a Turban to the wall
above my bed, so that she

can watch when I strip
for sleep, or for lying
back with a harrowing

novel, or a woman,
or my own sullen mind.
Gazing down now, always

about to speak, she seems
equally intimate and remote,
like the soul. I would say

she was never disappointed
in love, though whatever
became of her after posing

in this lucid window-glow is
anybody's guess. I like
to believe she lived long,

suffered well, and knew
deep joy. Yet I appeal
to her as she is,

hoping she'll teach me
my own open secret. Dear
dead girl: did he love you?

I'm tired of art, and choose
to think he loved you more
than your image, that my

happiness in your beauty
is more than just the sum
of the effects of light.

One of the Lost Moments

We sat isolated among the others.
Her feet were bare in summer sandals,
bare and lovely, that's what I whispered.
She crossed her legs . . . discreetly
touched a toe to my naked ankle.
We swayed like neighboring birches
whose branches wind had blown together.

When I close my eyes, I still hear leaves
weaving those wild shadows around me.

Summer Storm

After dark, a storm begins: lightning
jags over the mountains in silence;

but seconds later, a limping thunder—
the noise of fire after the fire's gone,

a hollow noise that roars in the bones—
the roar of love after love is gone:

thus in the storm she comes to tremble
against me again, and I'm falling again—

falling darkly through the night like rain.

Journey With Music

I'm driving backroads through farmland at midnight, the fields on both sides bare, town lights sprinkled in the middle distance—the far distance lost in darkness. "Love is not an emotion," John told me. "Emotions," he said, "inspire particular actions. But what specific actions does love require?" I let the radio music crackle in and out of its channel. No use twisting the knob: something inside is loose.

"Love," said John, "is a way of being. It includes emotions. Includes attitudes. It includes ideas." He said, "This is why we can never repress love. It absorbs the repression, which changes the relationship but doesn't destroy it." I click off the radio, and listen to the bad road rumble beneath the car, punishing the shocks. Then I crank the window down and let the loud wind flood over me. . . .

Here's her town, now. I've driven miles to drift by her house in the moonlight, afraid she'll be sleeping. And yes, all of the windows are dark. I steer by twice, then stop and—having no paper to write on—leave a book in her door.

Back on the highway the wind feels colder, and I roll my window up, turn on the radio. The music seethes in and out of my thoughts, and I try the knob awhile . . . then give up.

Something inside is loose, I think. *Something inside is broken.*

Vander Meer Crying Fowl

How a word, a silence, flays the heart
like a baked game hen! Exposing
the frail needlebones that carried,
in life, the wild flesh and its awkward
desires. Thus, her voice

on the phone—its hunger repressed
uneasily into choice etiquette: a proper
knife-and-fork tenderness. No longer
does Vander Meer wonder what nibbles
his will away: she, or time, or memory—

or if he minds being so deliciously eaten.
Better (he supposes) than growing fat
on the lie that we know what lasts. Better
than feeding love's dim dream of flight—love,
created and raised for slaughter.

DRUNK AGAIN IN THE DARK GRASS

The cricket noise is a foam
of salt, a devouring
wave . . . I can feel it!
I can feel it.

Ah, too much
cold beer tonight.

Yet this music is hungry,
somehow: black with hunger
and its intimate erosions.

How long it's fed on me!

But now I have crawled out
of my sleep, wanting you, wanting
the cricket behind my right eye
to shut up, its black wave to stop
breaking down in me. Look—
it's a shaggy pasture
in Nebraska, in the sandhills:
a fine, star-riddled August midnight.
I woke in my tent with the moon

drenching through, and wanted you,
and crawled out here to let
the blackness eat me.
But for once, love,
it isn't enough.

For once I want to listen
past the waves. To fall silent,
let moonlight soak me to the bone!

Look: the moon's sailing high
in its own healing glow
like your face
when you're sleeping.

How long I've loved it.

August 8: "Abstinence"

On the telephone, her voice
still kindles her spirit
in memory. Gone to my head—champagne
of her glance . . . liqueur of sex,
its hazelnut sweetness. . . .

Yet our words are clinical,
sobering. We've sworn off our love,
taken the cure . . . and toast
ourselves with chilled mineral water—
clear, bitter draught of "what's possible."

AUGUST 13

A hundred yards out waves lift, lean shoreward, break and dissolve. This line of shells and smooth pebbles marks the farthest reach of the foam. Beyond, shingle the sea mist has moistened. The little stones shine with a gray light that comes from all sides at once; they glisten with longing: the sea is so close! So close, its heartbeat huge in the ground.

And beyond the shingle, the cliffs I've dreamed of . . . ash and bramble blowing on the crags, their soaked leaves dripping . . . as if love were tied up and left thrashing in the rain. . . .

I pick up a shell (faint rose and creamy brown, streaked with black) and hold it to my ear. How far away and small my heart is! Not at all like the sea. And these stones—they may never be dragged out into the depths, but only be brushed by the mist. . . .

How foolish! To think I could simply walk here awhile, and forget you.

September 23

*Cinching my belt to the fourth
notch—and still it's loose!*

*(How many weeks now
since I've touched you?)*

OCTOBER 19

All day I hear
the phone not ringing
not bringing your lips
to my ear

November 10

Three days of weeping eaves and pulsing gutters;
wet red fruit sagging the stubborn crabtrees;
thick grass lapsing into autumn, its green
drenching back into the earth: I wonder
what it means . . . this peculiar downpour,
coming on hard the way love can come over you—
keen, insistent, a quickening freshness: too late.

December 22: "Withdrawal"

Her silence smashed the pain barrier,
thunderclap trailing an acrid cloud
through my heart. I'd like to breathe,
but can't. My jaw goes stone at the hinge.
Say what I feel? All words are trash
in my throat's choked swash;
emotion's current will not flow—
a standing pool where a jet's shadow
crawls . . . or some water-strider
darting its blind, brief, anxious way
across what looks like sky. . . . Nothing
of self that isn't swamp. No wonder
she soars over! I can't ask anyone down
into me—their strength would fail in ooze.
I myself only survive myself by holding
breath . . . just surfacing at night;
by day, staying under, not opening my eyes—
fearing the water's infectious blackness,
the ravenous mouths swimming by. . . .

A Dream

I know this bathroom doorway, though the light
flooding from the window's harsher than usual sun—
scream-bright. The air cotton in an aching ear.
Over the sink the beast is bent—stocky, choleric,
intent—shaving with a stone. *When he turns,*
I think, *I'll die.* Then he turns . . .
the back of his gourdy head in the mirror's
my face. . . . I can't move. Can't stop
staring at the bloodied cheek, the ponderous
tail, the glassed-in face half-shadowed by hair,
the red-rheumed eye that squints like a knife.
"You know what I want," he c̀roaks. And I fly awake
sweating . . . the answer shaking its fist in my throat.

A Wakeful Night

The moon edges out of the clouds, sharp
cry upon the mottled dark: I remember
dreaming that I'd seen it before—
but that hour and its meaning
are empty of me now. Here
is the back yard, the garden
beside the fruitless apple tree;
and there, on the house-wall,
my stranger shadow, a wash
of Buddhist ink. Yet the moon's
still a thorn in the windy sky's mind:
I dreamed I once had a name in its light.

Saint Vander Meer and the Dragon

Take the male praying mantis, eaten
by love, in love with his own
torment.
         Or the horned toad
lying flat in the weeds
like a syrup-soaked waffle, munching
his own young as their mother
looks on.
         Or the fox who thrashes,
trapped, for a day, maybe two—
before he must gnaw through his own
thighbone to freedom. . . .

                    Vander Meer
tosses fretfully on the bare ground
beyond sleep's wrought-iron gate,
knowing inside is a pillowing stone
with his name on it.

             Oh, he fears
sleep! For she comes to him in sleep.
"What I must do I will do," she whispers.
And he:

"I am lifting my shirt. Here—
touch this scar, curled like woodshaving
or a question mark. Feel underneath it
the beating hollow where my heart
once lay."
If her tender fingers find it,
he never knows (this is the meaning of
awakening) . . . he never knows.

                          And so
lifts up his shield, whose crest is
mantis, horned toad and fox;
its motto: "Life lives upon life."

Though cold, a kind of comfort.

RECALLING THE SOLSTICE

Grass and junipers gray with frost
just before dawn. The dark gray too,
with a mist drifted off the river.
(In language it seems symbolic,
but out my window it was only cold
cloudiness turned up hauntingly

over night.) I saw the bones
of the weeping birch bewildering
the air, and thought of her—
"lovely in her bones," as Roethke
would say. And I felt as crazy-sane
as him a moment, wanting a light

touch to keep her bearable
in mind. But the mist was heavy.
(My voice feels heavy, sinking
into the madness of print.) Winter
began to glow gray in the yard:
the sun was rising far away.

JANUARY 29

*I dream her waking, mother-of-pearl sky
through the uncurtained window....*

*(Perhaps, in reality, a hand
touches her hip—but it's* my *dream,
so her husband is absent.)*

*She slips out from under the comforter,
peignoir of bluegreen twilight ... quietly
over the carpet then, to the stairway,
and down to the kitchen.*

*The dark is underwater gloom (I hold
my breath), but then she flicks on
the faint stovehood lamp.... A mist
of blonde down gleams on the back of her neck,
her head tilts pensively over the heating kettle.*

As though she could hear me, I move my lips:
Body of a dolphin, breast of cloud....

*

I fear she wakes, in reality, touched
by his cynical hand . . . that she

slips out from under their covers,
slumps on the edge of the bed. I fear

she may gaze at that twilit sky—
mother-of-pearl, immaculate

blue of the dolphin—forgetting
it's the color of her eyes, that I

saw it there, and love it: a brightness
that deepens my shadow like morning light.

February 14: "Ghazal"

If your heart lacked strength for bearing grief,
why did you struggle so to share my sorrow?

Hiding from gossip behind a dusty veil?
You'd marry your secretive love to the grave.

Sworn vows gone into the ground with your love;
from us the world inherits nothing but dust.

That call avoids the ear, that vision the eye.
The lone heart staggers in a downpour of sorrow.

Our fervor never ripened to the color of madness.
Yet what prodigal longings still darken our hearts!

(After Ghalib)

February 20

*Windswept lakewater just before dawn, glacial,
mercurial . . . a pineshadowed turbulence.
This heart, Dear Absence, you've placed in me.*

February 23

At a crossroads, traffic blows by heavily;
a few poplars with my dreams inside them
stir as the traffic passes. That's why

there's a papery rustle in my chest
as we say goodbye (not parting slowly
anymore, like lovers, but in haste,

like tourists). And I find myself far
from home again; on their shallow roots,
the shadowy trees sway faintly as I pass.

February 28

The night I drove to you late, stars spattered
like milk above black fields the whole forty miles,
I cranked down the windows, letting nightsmells
thunder in: cattle-rich earth, moonsilvered water
flashing down furrows that fanned as I passed.
All the way I fought the motor's hypnosis—held
your face in mind . . . saw it shining through mist
over shadowy windrows of cottonwood and elm.
It's still your face that keeps me awake; seems
I write of little else—which wounds us all.
Yet I hammer my one theme like a sour churchbell.
If the faithful stay home, who can blame them?
My sermon's like dull travel photos—all scenery;
no moral, no vision . . . only this wandering memory.

March 10:
"From an Unmailed Letter"

My wife, happening upon my journal, said:
"Writers are crueler than normal people."
I argued. Yet, facing this page, I
do feel it: my willingness to wound you
with grief-sharpened praise, an impossibly
possible vision of our future in love—
when what you need, what I owe you,
is more merciful: my silence.

If I dream of awakening beside you,
why say it? Why mention some birdsong day
in June, fresh wind pouring a sweetness
of dust through the screens? Outside,
leaves twitter on twigs in the cloudlight,
their shadows bathing us . . . can you
feel it? Can you feel why I say it?
My will-'o-the-heart words. . . .

I would be kinder, but speech seduces me—
itself seduced by the baths of delight
our bodies drew for us. Am I cruel,
then? Draining our lives into language

*where even joy is suffering. . . ? My love,
I suffer words for the normal joy they redeem—
and therefore hope they'll make you suffer:
you, kinder than my heart can stand.*

The Ache

An arrowhead ache in the breastbone marrow—
her body in my mind again . . . eyes, lips,
the tender folds nestled in moist blonde hair.
Months I fought it. Now her memory fells me.
My flesh weighs me down like failed armor.
Yet how impeccably the arrow's stem
shoots up from my heart! How its feathers
flicker . . . brighter than poppies in the wind.

SNAPSHOTS

My fingers combing
your thick blonde hair

still can't let go
of that moment

*

Holding
your face

inches
away

simply
looking

*

Even now your breath at my ear
sound of the summer rain we loved

coming each time making the earth
whisper its yes all around us

*

Wind gusted
through screens

through your body
through mine

*

That month's like a peach cut in half
even the deep ragged wound is sweet

*

I felt in your body
the peach tree blossom

now its shade embraces me
branches out of reach

Vander Meer at Sundown

Cold wind brisk over broad lake water—
the shudder in Vander Meer's blood
as he reads: "The grave question
of how long positive values can endure
only as the aftershine of something
that has been lost."

Doing right, doing well—
morality and success—no soul
knows them! The soul distinguishes
nothing but the bright act from
the brighter . . . a desire
from its fulfillment.

Thinks Vander Meer, *All light's
receding from me like the galaxies.*
Too grand! The glints that needle
his stinging eyes aren't stars,
but a single star: 'Pollo Phoibee,
scattered red upon the broken waters.

BED OF COALS

I can't sleep, thinking about the amusement park
where I run The Calypso: thirty cars held to a hub
by hydraulic spokes whose festive lights flash
as the motor drives it all around. The great wheel
thunders clockwise for a minute, shudders, stops,
then for one more minute it thunders backward,
before the ride's over. And the passengers laugh
or scream, mouths wide as if gulping the garish air,
lifting their bare arms like pale spiders crushed
under a shoe, or the blonde hair that glistened
as she dozed with her legs apart, letting the June
windowlight and the breeze kiss her dry. I always
stare into the heart of the wheel as it turns,
until the shrieks recede, and the blaring music,
and I start to hear her breathing beyond the noise
as I can hear her now, though I'm quite alone—
sleepless, a bit dizzy, bound to the blazing spokes
as to a bed of coals. I feel the earth wheeling
when I toss like a flame on my bed of coals.

Vander Meer at Sea

Vander Meer happens on a note, in her
firm cursive. Directions: those he'd given
over the phone, the ones she'd followed,
that day she drove down from the mountains
to tell him she wanted her freedom.
                                        August,
wind brisk and hot. The park was nearby,
he had only an hour for lunch—and so
they sat in the long grass, under maples
thick with leaves . . . green shadows
breaking over them in waves. . . .
"I can't," she said. It was simple—
like a blunt gaff in the chest. "I just
can't. . . . Not right now. Not yet,"
she said. And he said he felt the same:
"It's my kid," he lied, thinking—
I am going to die. . . .
                        He didn't,
of course. Didn't die. But gazing down
at that quick blue scrawl, reading
her roundness in every curve,
the set of her jaw in each
grammarless dash . . . he feels

the paper's tidal blankness swelling
through the words . . . and his breath
coming harder, shallower, faster—
quietly slipping under. . . .

BLACK WATERS

A hushed sea-like throbbing under the fingernail moons,
fluting of bones tied in windy branches, a thrash of June leaves,
and the breath like a netted swallow when the loved one's face appears,
continual surge and spill drenching the shore's arching body.

O dreams of bondage where the dangling spider dances!
Dream of the lost hat, the twisted leg, a dream of shouting.
The cracked tooth dream and the dream of endless invisible error.
Dream of a child hanged, the sweet body buried in a flowerpot,
and the gnat's dream of being someone's soul at my ear.

If what flashes in the blood is not a threaded needle,
if it's not sleep and waking at war, but two kinds of sleep,
if the gray eyes rolling back into the helmet's shadow are my own,
if what flashes in the heart is the fang of a rattler. . . .

The ship with its back broken groans on the reef!
And the sea-foam blossoms and withers on the raw timbers.
And the bruised moon, blinded, wanders above the clouds alone.

The mouth opens, half closes, opens . . . the doomed mouth pulses,
the black waters rush freely in and out of it like speech. . . .

March 21:
"Elemental Prayer in a Black Hour"

1

Icy wind, lover-like mouth, drink down
this bitter cloud I took for a soul.
Sip it out through the bones of my ears
as a widow sucks tea through a sugar cube.

2

Carry off my shadow in your shadow's arms,
bleak river. Freeze me until I'm glass.
Let my failures flood and pass through me
like moonlight—leaving me empty, but clear.

3

Swallow my heart, sullen earth, and my eyes.
I bring them to you, their dreams intact,
as neophytes once offered you seeds of barley.
Feed them your darkness. Force their sweet fruit.

4

Huddled fire, comfort my flesh—and my mind,
"which is also flesh." Let my voice rise
like smoke. Let it drift as the night goes,
seasoning the day with the scent of vanishing.

Vander Meer at Bottom

Sunken like a river rock, Vander Meer reads
the ripples of light that passing cars
scrawl across his bedroom wall. No
breathing beside him . . . no child's
next door.
        Inside: a "critical vacancy,"
like that morning in seventh grade Science—
the frog in its wet steel pan, splayed
beneath the toylike blade in his
witless grasp. . . .

        Which brings to mind
Moreau's island horrors: the red-edged
paperback he thumbed apart that year.
Intrigued not by the beasts (the likes
of whom he knew from cruel locker rooms),
but by the Doc himself. How murderous
piecing lives together can become!

        Madness,
muses Vander Meer, *has always wooed me.*
Like the dark spring that emptied from him
into his blue notebook . . . shuddering,

kissing along the margins. How often
it spilled into nights like this! Nights
of wandering mindlessness . . . images
gushing forth, lovely and terrible
by turns. . . .

     *Let the headlights' babble
speak for me*, he thinks. *Let nothing
more flow from my own life.*
                       Yet he dreams
of a birch rod whistling down, striking
fountains from a stone.
                  Then wakes
with a cry in his throat: "Strike again!"
Oh yes. If the pain can tap such wells in me.

The Dazzle

The green hills must have bewitched the fog,
it touched them so obsessively (the way memory
weaves its witness over the absent face you love).
Overhead, morning bled through the sodden branches

as your body sweated out its ache; but the thought
of how that chill had seeped into you made you shake,
and shut your eyes, and listen to the massive waves
drumming against the headland. Perhaps you dozed,

for you've started alert with the sun suddenly hot
on your cheeks: tears spent, your breath relaxed.
The sea's cobalt now, sky all pearl; the naked
cliffs stand clear and jagged in the dazzle.

Awakenings

Out on the murky lake—what's that sail doing? It dips so far down the boat may be swamped, any second now, filling with waves. Waves that are somehow too big for this wind, which has rushed out of the mountains and been made faint by houses and office buildings . . . not the kind of wind that moves whole lakes. Yet the water's rough, restless, thrashing in its fitful dream, making the blue sail tip, the boat's rudder lift and slice the air.

And the fear that flashes in the boatman's eye is so familiar! Because all our awakenings are like this: the amateur captain inside us—who only wanted to waste time, to drift and relax—must drown in awakening . . . his little craft swirling into the depths. . . .

Only then does the lake grow calm and clear. So that even from shore we can watch the sleek fish feeding along the bottom, strong and ancient, gliding through the ravel and weave of muddy water weeds.

FULLNESS

Living on beer and coffee, we
burned off ten pounds each in half
as many weeks (in love, the body
grows lean to feed the heart).
Now, months later, I still
dream the floodstream surge
and twist of your torso, soft
turn of the pelvic hollows
I kissed against thirst—
and my tongue goes on swimming
its bloodwarm waters into speech:
for what? My network of lines
spirals out . . . sinks
in the cold lake stretching
between us, while I keep
trying to swallow the fishbone
moments of the past—as if
I could live on loss.
Yet it isn't loss,
but fullness recalled
to fullness again: my heart
no starveling, though it hurts—
aches like a bulging net
I strain to raise: memories
hauled up over and over, quick
and seething in the drowning air.

THE WOUND

A fresh-fallen limb, the blossoms still on—
dim stars amid the restless green. Interrupting
my therapeutic morning walk, I bent over it,
touched the tender inner wood where the branch
had fastened to its trunk.
                Lightning?
                              Or a wind?
The limb was long, slender, smoothly tapered.
Felled by its own weight then? My fingers
crept across the moist white wound.
What a frail grain!
                That could not bear
to bear such a profusion of flowers and leaves.

Vander Meer's Duplicity

Vander Meer at the mirror, mouth
propped wide with a gunbarrel
index finger, thinking:
"easeful death" . . . playing
homo ludens to the hilt. Who was it
said, a good poem always takes
the top of one's head off?

Gruesome Vander Meer! Not a little
tired of getting so weird. Peers
to find the tooth that stabs
his sleep—but as ever the ache's
general in his jaw, as if he'd chewed
his tongue's bloody rag all night.
Look, mirror-man whispers, *such
morbidity's a sign of decay:
mental* . . . scolding with a dogtail
wag of his finger. No no no *no,*
like Beethoven said. . . .

Bitter Vander Meer. Half in love
with this new life alone with his art
(a cracked memoir he calls *Bed of Coals*),

half with a dream of being gathered
into artless eternity—from which sleep
what holds him back? One truth:
his heart's not in it.

BEYOND SORROW

In the crowd a girl's face
not yours but eyes
like yours

hour-before-dawn
cloudless summer sky

where I'd rather
vanish like the moon
than burn without light
the way I do

my voice
a wind that carries toward you
stinging briarsmoke words
my grief

*

I don't want to go on
grieving like a thawing rock
bleeding snowmelt and ghostly steam

I don't want to go on gnawing
my heart like a charred bone

I don't want to go on as an open eye
that visions of your body rain
into like sweet acid

*

enough to fade
like a moon drowned in morning light
or to shine only in the dark
behind your eyes

enough now
to love you in other faces
and feel my heart silently rise
inside me
may that rising speak
inside you as well

luminous pulse
like an ocean underground
my joy constant beyond sorrow

Chinook at Midnight

This gust from the screen that quickens
my skin, with its fragrance of lilacs
and the opulence of high, backlit clouds,
makes me close my eyes and rock, bough-like,
holding a face in mind.

                      Always your face—
you . . . white moon amid the ragged leaves
that rustle like a pulse in my ear. Your light
comes down, I might say, brokenly; but truth
is, the wind scatters it over my longing

like manna, like a balm of blossoms.

THE VOICE OF REASON

The error, of course, is thinking
there's a way to live your life,
as one might "drive a car." Life
is what drives *you*. Such a stinking

shame . . . having so little control!
And yet all the time resisting it—
control, I mean. You'd *love* to quit
sweating like some gambler on a roll,

but not enough to drop your dice.
You throw. You throw again. You
throw until your lips go blue,
blowing on cubes of acrylic ice

like the embers of your joy (these
are what you dream will some day
light your road—or so you say).
My guess is you'll finally freeze

in this posture of blind expectancy.
And I think you'll learn that life
reveals only what it was: *your* life,
as headlong and as aimless as the sea.

This Day

On the corner, anachronistic in mid-October,
a girl in jogging shorts . . . tanned legs
glistening with sparse, honey-pale down,
her thighs strong, smooth as buttered rum.

How keep from staring through her to find you?

I look away, I rush past . . . but the wind
breathes at my ear until I taste your tongue,
dream your breasts, fingers, subtle waist—
whispers from my book of hours.
                              All
that time scatters, memory gathers up—
keepsakes, relics, talismans. I touch one
after another like lines of print or furrows
in a face: my face, seventy . . . held up
by fear like a rust-flecked mirror. Did years
ravage that brow? Or the lash of your loss?
Do I wake even then with this emptiness
kneeling on my heart?
                        My own eyes
stare through me!
                I look away.
                          Rush past.

Yet, in flight, I blunder into it. This day:
autumn surging in the veins of each leaf,
tangled clouds above shadowy mountains,
the morning sun dazzling, remote, eternal—

how all we love will look to us, looking back.